Read

- Descriptions in this manual are based on what is available at the time of writing this guide, and it may not be 100% accurate again if there is a major software update to All-New Echo Dot (2nd Generation).

- All information supplied in this guide is for educational purpose only and users bear the responsibility for using it.

- Although I took tremendous effort to ensure that all information provided in this guide are correct, I will welcome your suggestions if you find out that any information provided in this guide is inadequate or you find a better way of doing some of the actions mentioned in this guide. All correspondence should be sent to pharmibrahimguides@gmail.com

About This Guide

Finally, a concise, straightforward and succinct manual on All-New Echo Dot (2nd Generation) for newbies, seniors, students, instructors and tech lovers is here. This is the guide Amazon should have included in the box.

I know you have a lot of things to do and you will not want to be bothered by irrelevant things, so I have made this manual to be very concise and straightforward. Interestingly, it is a step-by-step manual so you can be confident that you will understand the information contained inside it.

PS: Please make sure you don't give the gift of All-New Echo Dot (2nd Generation) without given this companion guide alongside with it. This guide makes your gift a complete one.

Table of Contents

How to Use This Guide

This guide is an unofficial manual of All-New Echo Dot (2nd Generation) and it should be used just like you use any reference book or manual.

To quickly find a topic, please use the table of contents. This will allow you to quickly find information and save time.

You don't need to stick to commands given in this manual. In fact, you can say all the example commands given in this guide in another ways; the most important thing is to get Echo Dot to understand what you are saying.

Lastly, I have based the descriptions in this manual on the assumption that you will be controlling your Echo Dot using the wake word "Alexa". However, if you are using another wake word, you can get the same result just by replacing "Alexa" with the wake word you are using.

I hope this guide helps you get the most out of your Echo Dot.

Introduction

Echo Dot is a low price, but functionally similar version of Amazon Echo. Echo Dot is about 1.3 inches tall making it slightly shorter than the first generation Echo Dot. This guide will show you how to manage Echo Dot like a pro and how to ask questions and give commands that Echo Dot will understand.

Unpacking Your Device

When you unpack your product box, check your product box for the following items:

1. Echo Dot
2. USB charging cable
3. Power adapter (9W)
3. Quick Start Guide

Get to know your device

Device Layout of Echo Dot (2nd Generation)

Number	Function
1.	Volume Up Button
2.	Action Button: This button can be used to wake your device, turn off a timer or alarm and enable Wi-Fi setup mode. To use the Action button to enable Wi-Fi mode press and hold it for about five seconds.
3.	Light Ring: This tells you about the device's status.
4.	Volume Down Button
5.	Microphone Button: Press this button to turn off the microphones. When this microphone is off, the light ring turns red. To turn on the microphone again, press this button again.
6.	7-Microphone Array
7.	AUX audio output (3.5mm): Use this port to connect Echo Dot to larger speakers
8.	Micro-USB port: Use this port to connect Echo Dot with the included power cable.

Different Light Ring Statuses

Light ring tells you many things about your device.

- When the light ring is not showing any light (but it is connected to a power source), then your device is active and waiting for your request.
- Solid blue with cyan pointing in direction of person speaking means Alexa is busy processing your request.
- Orange light spinning clockwise means your device is connecting to your Wi-Fi network.
- Solid blue with spinning cyan lights means your device is starting up.
- Solid red light means the microphones on your device is turned off.
- A blinking orange light means that your Echo Dot is connected to your Wi-Fi network, but can't access the Alexa Voice Service.
- White light means you are adjusting the volume level on your device.

Turning your Echo Dot on and off

Just like many other smart devices, turning on your device is as simple as ABC. To turn on your Echo Dot, just connect it to a power output using the power adapter that came with it. The light ring on Echo Dot turns blue, and then orange. When the light turns orange, Alexa greets you.

Please note that you may not get your Echo Dot to work using phone or tablet chargers. I will advise that you always connect your Echo Dot to a power outlet using the power adapter and USB cord that came with it.

To turn off Echo Dot, unplug it from the power source.

Tip: It is recommended to place your Echo Dot at least 20cm or eight inches from any walls and windows.

Getting started with Echo Dot

You will need to setup Echo Dot when you first start using it and you will learn how to do that in this section of the guide. To setup Echo Dot you will need the following things:

1. Echo Dot
2. Internet Access through a Wi-Fi Network
3. A tablet or phone with Alexa app. You can also access the Alexa app using your computer's browser if you don't want

to install this app. Please note that to install Alexa app, you will need either of these:

    a. Fire OS 2.0 or higher

    b. Android 4.0 or higher

    c. iOS 7.0 or higher

Alexa app is free and you can download it from the Google Play Store, Amazon App Store or Apple App Store. All you need to do is to go to one of this app store, search for **Amazon Alexa App** and tap the download button. Then tap **Begin Setup** and follow the prompts.

To setup Echo Dot:

1. Connect Echo Dot to a power output using the power adapter that came with it. Echo Dot then light up automatically and tell you it is ready for setup.

2. Open Alexa app. I assumed you have installed Alexa app following the instructions above. Alternatively, go to **http://alexa.amazon.com** using computer's browser. Supported browser include from Safari, Chrome, Firefox and Microsoft Edge. For the purpose of descriptions, I will assume that you are controlling/setting up your Echo Dot using the Alexa app installed on your tablet or phone. However, if you are controlling/ setting up your Echo Dot using a web browser, you can still follow similar steps described in this manual.

3. In the Alexa app, tap **Begin Setup** or tap the menu button ▤ located at the top left corner of the screen and then tap **Settings**. If you are using Fire tablet, you can access the menu by swiping in from the left edge of the screen.

4. On the Alexa app screen, select your device **(Echo Dot)** from the list.

5. On the Alexa app screen, choose a Language (if required) and tap **Continue.**

6. On the Alexa app screen, select **Connect Wi-Fi**.

7. On your Echo Dot, wait for this device to tell you that it is ready and the Light ring will turn Orange. If this process does not occur automatically, press the action button (the dot button) for few seconds. The light ring on the Echo Dot should change to orange and the Echo Dot will connect to your phone/tablet.

8. On the Alexa app screen, tap **Continue.** Alexa app will then tell you that it is **attempting to connect to Echo.** This may take some time. A confirmation message appears in the app when it is connected to your Echo Dot.

9. On the Alexa app screen, tap **Continue**. A list of available Wi-Fi networks then appear in the app, tap on a Wi-Fi network. Enter a password for the network (if necessary) and tap on **Connect/Join**. If you don't see your network, tap **Rescan** or manually add the network by tapping **Add a Network** (if you are using a Fire tablet). Please note that you will need to manually add a *hidden* Wi-Fi network.

10. Then wait for the Echo Dot to connect to a Wi-Fi network. After your device connects to your Wi-Fi network, a confirmation message appears in the app. Tap **Continue** to allow your Echo Dot to perform a system update (if necessary). That is all, you have now setup your Echo Dot and it is ready for use.

To go to Alexa App Home, Just tap **Continue/Next** until you see **Go to Home.** You can perform many tweaks on Echo Dot using the Alexa App. More on this shortly.

If you are using the Alexa app for the first time, you may be shown advert as you try to navigate the Alexa app, to close any of these advert, tap **No thanks** or the **X** icon.

Note:

When your Echo Dot is connected to a Wi-Fi network, it should give a solid white light. A solid orange light means your Echo Dot is not connected to your Wi-Fi network. In addition, a blinking orange light means that your Echo Dot is connected to your Wi-Fi network, but can't access the Alexa Voice Service.

Tip: You can follow similar steps mentioned above to update your Wi-Fi network on Echo Dot. However, on step 6 above, choose **Update Wi-Fi.**

Troubleshooting Wi-Fi Connection when using Alexa App or Echo Dot

Echo Dot or Alexa App may sometimes refuse to process your request or connect the Wi-Fi network. When this happens, you may try any of the suggestions below:

1. Make sure you don't have limited network connectivity in that area. If your network is good and you still cannot connect, you may perform any of these actions.

   • Try restarting the Wi-Fi.

   • Move closer to your router and scan for the available networks. If the network still does not shows up, you may add the network manually.

   • Restart your router and modem. Unplug the modem and router for few minutes and plug the modem in and then the router.

   • Unplug your Echo Dot from the power source, wait for few seconds and plug it back.

   • If your phone/tablet is not connecting to the internet, make sure the Flight Mode is off. To check whether Flight mode is enabled, swipe down from the top of the screen if you are using an Android or Fire OS. Flight Mode icon ✈ will appear bold when enabled/on. Please note that the Flight mode should be disabled/off to access wireless networks.

- Try restarting you phone/tablet.

Connecting Echo Dot to a Wi-Fi/Mobile Hotspot

For one reason or the other you may want to use your phone as a hotspot and connect your Echo Dot to it. Doing this is quite simple and it is discussed below:

1. Turn on the hotspot feature on your phone. Please refer to your phone's manual if you don't know how to activate this feature. In addition, please note that you may incur some extra charges while using your phone as a hotspot.

2. While the Echo Dot is connected to a power source and working, open the Alexa app on your mobile device.

3. In the Alexa app, tap the menu button located at the top left corner of the screen and then tap **Settings**. If you are using Fire tablet, you can access the menu by swiping in from the left edge of the screen.

4. On the Alexa app screen, select your device **(Echo Dot)** from the list and then select **Update Wi-Fi**.

5. On your Echo Dot, wait for this device to tell you that it is ready and the Light ring will turn Orange. If this process does not occur automatically, press the action button (the dot button) for few seconds. The light ring on the Echo Dot

should change to orange and the Echo Dot will connect to your phone/tablet.

6. A list of available Wi-Fi networks then appear in the app, tap the name of a network corresponding to your mobile hotspot, enter the password and tap **Connect** and wait for the connection to be established.

7. If you can't see the name of your mobile hotspot, scroll down on the Alexa app and select **Use this device as a Wi-Fi hotspot.**

8. Tap on **Start**.

9. Enter your Wi-Fi hotspot's network name and password and tap on **Connect**.

10. Then wait for the Echo Dot to connect to a Wi-Fi hotspot. After your device connects to your Wi-Fi hotspot network, Alexa then confirms a successful connection.

11. That is all. You can now ask Alexa what you will like it to do.

Change the Wake Word

To get the attention of Echo Dot you will need to say the wake word followed by the command.

Amazon allows you to choose between Alexa, Echo, or Amazon

To change your wake word:

1. While the Echo Dot is connected to a power source and working, open the Alexa app on your mobile device.

2. In the Alexa app, tap the menu button ☰ located at the top left corner of the screen and then tap **Settings**. If you are using Fire tablet, you can access the menu by swiping in from the left edge of the screen.

3. Select your device (Echo Dot) from the menu.

4. Scroll down and select **Wake Word**.

5. Tap the drop-down menu to select a wake word, and then tap **Save**. When you change the wake word, the light ring on your device should flash orange briefly.

6. Say your new wake word followed by a command to test if everything is ok.

Connecting Echo Dot to Bluetooth Devices

Interestingly, Echo Dot is Bluetooth enabled meaning that you can connect it to other Bluetooth enabled devices like your phone or external speaker.

If after following steps mentioned in this guide you are not able to connect an external Speaker to your Echo Dot, it may be that the speaker is not supported. You can check out the list of certified Bluetooth speakers for Echo Dot (2nd Generation) here **https://www.amazon.com/b?node=14048078011**.

In addition, Echo Dot can be connected to an external speaker using 3.5 mm audio cable that is sold separately.

Connecting Echo Dot to a Mobile Bluetooth Device

You can connect Echo Dot to mobile devices like phones and tablets. In this case, your Echo Dot will be acting as external speaker. However, please note that Alexa doesn't receive or read phone calls, text messages, and other notifications from your mobile device.

To connect your Echo Dot to a Bluetooth enabled mobile device:

1. While the Echo Dot is connected to a power source and working, open the Alexa app on your mobile device.

2. In the Alexa app, tap the menu button located at the top left corner of the screen and then tap **Settings**. If you are using Fire tablet, you can access the menu by swiping in from the left edge of the screen.

3. Select your Echo Dot from the list and then select **Bluetooth**

4. Tap **Pair a New Device**. Your Echo Dot then enters pairing mode.

5. On your mobile device, navigate to Bluetooth settings, and select your **Echo Dot**. If you don't see Echo Dot in the list, try rescanning for new devices. Alexa then tells you if the connection is successful.

6. To disconnect your mobile device from Echo Dot, say, **Alexa Disconnect**.

7. To connect to this mobile device again or a previously paired device, say **Alexa Connect My Mobile Device (or Alexa Pair My Mobile Device)**. Echo Dot will then connect to the device that was last connected.

Please note that you will need to disconnect your Echo Dot before you can connect it to another device. Echo Dot can only connect a single device at a time.

You can control the volume of your device by pressing the volume keys (- or + keys) on the Echo Dot. Alternatively, to control the volume you may say **Alexa** followed by a volume number. For example, you may say **Alexa volume 7.** You may also say **Alexa turn on/down the volume.**

Connecting Echo Dot to a Bluetooth Speaker

You can connect Echo Dot to a Bluetooth speaker. In this case, the Bluetooth speaker will be acting as external speaker.

To connect Echo Dot to a Bluetooth speaker:

1. Turn on pairing mode on your Bluetooth speaker. You can easily do this by referring to the user guide that came with your Bluetooth speaker.

2. While the Echo Dot is connected to a power source and working, open the Alexa app on your mobile device.

3. In the Alexa app, tap the menu button located at the top left corner of the screen and then tap **Settings**. If you are using Fire tablet, you can access the menu by swiping in from the left edge of the screen.

4. Select your Echo Dot from the list and then select **Bluetooth**

5. Tap **Pair a New Device**. Your Echo Dot then enters pairing mode.

6. Echo Dot searches for Bluetooth devices, and then the external speaker appears in the list of available of devices in the Alexa app.

7. Select your Bluetooth speaker. You will get a confirmation message from Alexa when your Echo Dot connects to the speaker.

8. In the Alexa app select **Continue**.

9. To disconnect your speaker from Echo Dot, say, **Alexa Disconnect**.

10. To connect to this speaker again or a previously paired device, say **Alexa Connect My Bluetooth Speaker (or Alexa Pair My Bluetooth Speaker)**. Echo Dot will connect to the device that was last connected.

Please note that you will need to disconnect your Echo Dot from a speaker before you can connect it to another device. Echo Dot can only connect a single device at a time.

You can control the volume of your device by pressing the volume keys (- or + keys) on the Echo Dot or the volume the keys on your external speaker. Alternatively, to control the volume you may say **Alexa** followed by a volume number. For example, you may say **Alexa volume 7.** You may also say **Alexa turn on/down the volume.**

Using Echo Dot with IFTTT

IFTTT (If This Then That) is an online service that allows you to automate different actions. Although Alexa can perform a lot of tasks but it can't do everything. Connecting your Alexa device to IFTTT allows you to perform some actions that may not be possible with Alexa alone. With the help of IFTTT, Echo Dot can be used with third-party control devices that are not officially supported.

To connect Echo Dot to IFTTT:
1. From your web browser go to ifttt.com
2. Click on **Sign in**, if you don't have an account click on **Sign up**.

3. Enter the necessary information and click Sign in or Sign up.

4. Click on **Channels** located at the top of the screen.

5. Search for **Amazon Alexa.** The list filters as you type. Click on **Amazon Alexa.**

6. Click on **Connect.**

7. Enter your Amazon login information and click on **Sign In.** Amazon will then show you what it will share, click on **Okay** to accept.

Using IFTTT

After you have connected Amazon Alexa and IFTTT, you will need to choose some recipes. Recipes are simple conditional statements which are triggered based on what you tell Alexa to do.

For example, you may choose a recipe that allows you to receive an email with your complete Shopping list in your Gmail account when you ask Alexa to review your Shopping list. To do this, while on Amazon Alexa channel page, just click on the icon show below and follow the onscreen instructions.

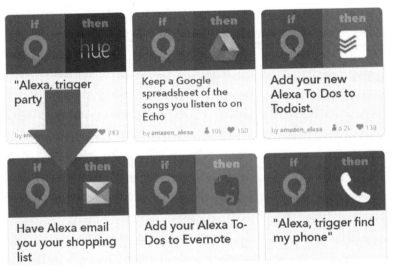

Tip: After activating this recipe, you can get an email of your shopping list just by saying **Alexa, what's is on my shopping list?**

Using Echo Dot with Different Types of Skills

You can give a new set of skills to your Echo Dot using the Alexa app. So what is a skill? A skill is a special action performed by Echo Dot when it is connected to another device, app, website or item. For example, you can give Echo Dot some extra mathematical skills by connecting it to a third party app called **Math Puzzle.** In addition, you can give Echo Dot some flight information capabilities by connecting it to a third party app called **KAYAK.** Furthermore, you can give Echo Dot some smart control capabilities by connecting it to a skill called **SmartThings**.

In a nutshell, connecting a skill to Echo Dot transforms the way you use this device. It lets you do what you can't do with Echo Dot alone. In this section of the guide, you will be learning the basic steps to follow to connect a new skill to Echo Dot.

To add a skill to Echo Dot:

1. Open Alexa app and tap on the menu icon located at the top left corner of the screen.

2. Tap on **Skills**

3. Tap on **Categories** and choose a category and then a skill. Alternative, tap the Search bar located at the top of the screen and enter a search phrase.

4. Tap a skill and follow the onscreen instructions to link this skill to Echo Dot. Please note that you may be required to enter some account information to link a skill.

5. You are now ready to use the new skill.

Tip: To link a smart home device, just follow the steps 1 to 3 above and tap on **Smart Home** category. Then choose a skill and follow the prompts to enable this skill.

In addition, you may be able to enable/disable some skills using your voice. For example, you may say:

- **Alexa, enable Kayak**
- **Alexa, disable Kayak**

Hint: Do you want to use Echo Dot in a special way? Then add nice Skills to it. You can know how to use a particular Skill by reading the information on the details page of the Skill.

Connecting Your Smart Devices to Echo Dot

You can link many smart home devices by following the steps mentioned on page 19. However, not all smart home devices can be linked by following the steps mentioned on page 19. Some devices simply require you to have Echo search for them on your network and connect with them. To link those devices that don't require a skill:

1. Open Alexa app and tap on the menu icon located at the top left corner of the screen.

2. Tap on **Smart Home.**

3. Scroll down to **Your Devices** and tap on **Discover Devices.** You may avoid these first three steps and just tell your Echo Dot to discover devices connected to your network by saying, **Alexa Discover Devices.**

4. Alexa app will then begin scanning your network for any connected smart home devices. In the case of the Philips Hue system, any application or device (including Alexa app) that wants access to the Hue bridge requires you tap the physical button on the Hue bridge in order to authorize it. But other smart home products (like Belkin WeMo devices) will not require any physical tapping. So if you are using a Philips Hue system, make sure you tap the physical button on the Hue bridge before you tap the **Discover Devices** button on the Alexa app.

5. Then you will see the list of all discovered devices on the Alexa app. Tap **Forget** next to a device's name to prevent Echo Dot from controlling the device or to remove the device. Please note that if a device does not appear under the discovered devices list, it may be that you will need to install the skill for the device instead. To install a skill for a smart home device, please go to page 19.

6. You are now ready to use your smart home devices with Echo Dot. But before you do that there is one more important thing to do and that is grouping your devices.

Tip: If after following the steps mentioned in this guide Echo Dot can't still discover your device, check the companion app for your smart home device to ensure that it's on the same Wi-Fi network as your Echo Dot.

In addition, please note that if you turn off or unplug your smart home device and then turn it back on, it may take some time before Alexa can rediscover the device

Grouping Your Smart Home Devices

Grouping your smart home devices allow you to control Echo Dot smartly. For example, you can create a group and name it **bedroom light** so that Echo Dot can access them whenever you make a command and you include bedroom light in the command. Please note that Echo Dot may not recognize any group you have created on your smart home device and you may need to create new groups using Alexa app.

To create a group:

1. Open Alexa app and tap on the menu icon ▤ located at the top left corner of the screen.
2. Tap on **Smart Home**
3. Under **Group,** Tap **Create Group.**
4. Enter the group name in the field provided. Give your group a recognizable name for Alexa to identify. For example, you

may use the name **Living Room light** to denote the light bulbs in your living room

5. Select the smart home device(s) you want to add to the group, and then select **Add/Save**.

To edit/manage a group:

1. Open Alexa app and tap on the menu icon ▤ located at the top left corner of the screen.
2. Tap on **Smart Home**
3. Under **Groups**, select your smart home group.
4. Make the necessary changes by tapping the required field.
5. To add or remove smart home devices, select the checkboxes next to each device.
6. To delete a group, tap **Delete.**

Communicating With Echo Dot

Speaking to Echo Dot

One of the ways you will interact with Echo Dot is by saying your questions. To get Echo Dot into action, you will need to get its attention. To do that, say the wake word followed by the command e.g. **Alexa, what is on my calendar today.**

Getting What You Want From Echo Dot

There are many things you can ask Echo Dot to do for you and before you finish reading this guide you will learn how to effectively interact with it.

I will like to mention that interacting with Echo Dot is not an examination (so there is nothing like cheating) and you get help by saying **Alexa, help**.

Using Echo Dot with Smart Home Devices

You can use Echo Dot to control your smart home devices. This is particularly interesting; imagine telling Alexa to turn on/off the light with just a voice command.

I will assume that you have already connected you smart home devices to your Echo Dot using the instructions provided on page 20. After connecting your smart home device to Echo Dot, then try any of these example commands:

- Alexa, turn on/off (smart home device/group name). For example, you may say **Alexa, turn off bedroom light**.

- Alexa, brighten/dim (smart home device/group name). For example, you may say **Alexa, brighten my living room light.** You may also say **Alexa, set my living room light to maximum**.

- Alexa set (smart home device/group name) temperature to (lower/higher) degrees. For example, you may say **Alexa, set Samsung thermostat to 20 degrees.**

- Alexa, set (smart home device/group name) to "x". For example, you may say **Alexa, Ling room fan to 5.**

Note: As I have said before, you will need to connect your smart home devices to your Echo Dot before you can use your Echo Dot to control these devices. To learn how to connect your Echo Dot to your smart device, please go to page 20.

Tip: Some smart home skills may support other device actions. To know what actions is supported go to the smart home skill in the Alexa app. To do this:

1. Open Alexa app and tap on the menu icon located at the top left corner of the screen.
2. Tap on **Skills**
3. Tap on **Categories** and tap **Smart Home.** Then read the descriptions under each skill.

Using Echo Dot with Your Calendar

One of the fantastic features that Echo Dot can do for you is making an appointment.

With just few commands you can get Echo Dot to put an event or appointment into your calendar. But before you can populate your calendar with events, you will need to first link your calendar with your Echo Dot. To do this:

Please note that you may need to setup a Google calendar at **https://calendar.google.com** (if you don't already have one) before you can complete the steps mentioned below.

1. Open Alexa app and tap on the menu icon located at the top left corner of the screen.

2. Tap on **Settings**

3. Tap on **Calendar** and select **Google Calendar**

4. Select **Link Google Calendar account** and follow the prompts.

5. To unlink your calendar at a future time, tap **Unlink Google Calendar account.**

After linking your Google Calendar to Echo Dot, you may try the following commands.

- **Alexa, what is on my calendar tomorrow?**
- **Alexa add an event to my calendar.**
- **Alexa, how does my calendar look like today?**
- **Alexa, add meeting with Clinton to my calendar for Friday at 6 a.m.**
- **Alexa add an appointment with Steve for Monday at 1 p.m.**

Please note that you can also say all the examples given above in another ways, the most important thing is to get Echo Dot to understand what you are saying.

Using Echo Dot with Your Shopping List and To-do List

There are probably many things going through your mind and it will be quite interesting if you can get a personal assistant to assist in putting it down inside a list. Fortunately, Echo Dot can help you in this regard.

To a add an item to your to-do list or shopping list, try any of the following commands:

- **Alexa, add 'go to my in-law house' to my to-do list**
- **Alexa, add (item) to my shopping list**
- **Alexa, what's on my shopping list**
- **Alexa, what's on my to-do List?**

Tip: If your Echo Dot is not nearby and you want to manage your shopping or to-do list, all you have to do is to:

1. Open Alexa app and tap on the menu icon located at the top left corner of the screen.
2. Tap on **Shopping & To-do Lists**.
3. Select either list.
4. To add a new item to the list, tap the plus icon "+"

5. To delete an item from a list, tap the **V** icon next to the list you want to delete and tap **Delete item**. Alternatively, mark the checkbox next to an item and select **Delete.**

In addition, you can print your list if you are accessing Alexa app from a computer, to access Alexa app from a computer, go to http://alexa.amazon.com. Then in the left navigation menu click **Shopping & To-do Lists.** Choose either list. Then select **Print.** Furthermore, you can link a third-party To-Do lists so that Echo Dot can make your Shopping List and To-do List available in third-party services. To do this:

1. Open Alexa app and tap on the menu icon located at the top left corner of the screen.
2. Tap on **Settings**.
3. Tap **Lists**.
4. Tap **Link** to the right of either Any.do or Todoist.
5. Enter your login information for the third-party service or create a new account and then follow the onscreen instructions to complete the linking process.

Using Echo Dot with Alarm

You can also set an alarm using this personal assistant. To do this, try these example commands:

- **Alexa, set an alarm for 1 p.m. tomorrow**
- **Alexa, set an alarm for 30 minutes from now.**

Tip: To stop the alarm when it is sounding, say **Alexa, stop the alarm**. You may also say **Alexa, snooze the alarm.** This will snooze the alarm for a particular period of time.

To set a repeating alarm, try this:

- **Alexa, set an everyday alarm for 7 a.m.**

To know the status of your alarm, try these:

- **Alexa, what time is my alarm set for?**
- **Alexa, what alarms do I have for Monday?**

To edit/delete an alarm use the Alexa app. To do this:

- Open Alexa app and tap on the menu icon located at the top left corner of the screen.
- Tap on **Timers & Alarms.**
- Choose your device from the drop-down menu.
- Select the **Alarms** tab.
- Choose the alarm you want to delete, and then select **Delete alarm**.

To change your alarm volume/sound:

1. Open Alexa app and tap on the menu icon ☰ located at the top left corner of the screen.
2. Tap on **Settings**
3. Select your device.
4. Tap **Sounds.**
5. To control the alarm volume, tap and drag the volume bar for **Alarm and Timer Volume**.
6. To change your alarm sound, select **Alarm Default Sounds**, and then pick a new sound.
7. To change the sound for a particular alarm, select the alarm you want to edit. Select **Alarm Sound**, and then pick a new sound.

Using Echo Dot with Timer

You can set a timer using this personal assistant. To do this, try these example commands:

- **Alexa, set a timer 30 minutes.**
- **Alexa, set the timer for 3 p.m.**

Tip: To stop the timer when it is sounding, say **Alexa, stop the timer**.

To know the status of your timer, try this:

- **Alexa, how much time is left on my timer?**

To edit/delete a timer:

1. Open Alexa app and tap on the menu icon ☰ located at the top left corner of the screen.
2. Tap on **Timers & Alarms.**
3. Choose your device from the drop-down menu.
4. Select the **Timers** tab.
5. Select **Edit** next to the timer you want to stop, and then tap **Cancel**.

Tip: You can also use your voice to delete an upcoming timer, just say **Alexa cancel the timer for (amount of time).**

To change your timer volume:

1. Open Alexa app and tap on the menu icon ☰ located at the top left corner of the screen.
2. Tap on **Settings**
3. Select your device.
4. Tap **Sounds.**
5. Tap and drag the volume bar for **Alarm and Timer Volume**.

Using Echo Dot with Clock

You can ask Echo Dot what your local time is. In addition, it can also tell you the time in a specific place. To do this, try these example commands:

- **Alexa what is the time?**
- **Alexa what is the time in New York?**

Using Echo Dot to Get Flight Information

You can also use this personal assistant to get information about a flight. This is a smarter way to know when a particular airplane will take off. To do this you may need to connect Echo Dot to a skill called **Kayak.** To do this:

1. Open Alexa app and tap on the menu icon located at the top left corner of the screen.
2. Tap on **Skills**
3. Type **Kayak** into the search bar located at the top of the screen.
4. Tap **Kayak** and follow the onscreen instructions to link this skill to Echo Dot

That is it; you have now given your Echo Dot some new capabilities. Now you can ask Alexa some flight related questions like:

Alexa, ask Kayak when the flight from New York will arrive.

Alexa ask Kayak what is the flight status of Delta 400?

Listen to Your Audiobooks

Alexa can read audiobooks to you.

To read an audiobook you own, try any of these:

- **Alexa, read (title)**
- **Alexa, play the book, (title)**
- **Alexa ,read the audiobook, (title)**

To pause an audiobook, simply say **Alexa, Pause.** To resume, say **Alexa, resume my audiobook.**

To go back or forward in the audiobook by 30 seconds, say **Alexa, go back/forward**

To go to the next or previous chapter in an audiobook, say **Alexa, next chapter** or **Alexa, previous chapter**.

Say **Alexa, go to chapter 4** to go to a specific chapter.

To stop reading in a future time, say **Alexa stop reading the book in (x) minutes/hours.** Where x represents a number.

Read Kindle Books with Alexa

Alexa can read eligible Kindle books using text-to-speech technology.

To read a Kindle book you own, try any of these:

- **Alexa, read my Kindle book (title)**
- **Alexa, play the book (title)**
- **Alexa, read my book (title)**

To pause a Kindle book, simply say **Alexa, Pause.** To resume, say **Alexa, resume my Kindle book.**

To go next or previous paragraph in a Kindle book, say **Alexa, go back/forward**

Buying Items Using Your Voice

If you are a Prime member, you can talk to Echo Dot to order an item for you. To do this, you will first need to

1. Open Alexa app and tap on the menu icon located at the top left corner of the screen.
2. Tap on **Settings**
3. Tap **Voice Purchasing**
4. Tap an option:

a. **Purchase by voice**: Use the option to enable or disable voice purchasing

b. **(Optional) Require confirmation code:** This option allows you to enter a 4-digit code which Alexa will ask for before you complete a purchase. Interestingly, this code does not appear in your voice history.

c. **Manage 1-Click settings**: Use this option to update your 1-Click payment method and billing address.

After this setup, you may shop for Prime-Eligible items from Amazon using your voice. To order a product, you may say:

Alexa, order me (item name)

To reorder an item say **Alexa, reorder (item name)**

Please note that when ordering an item, you Alexa may ask you some questions, just say Yes/No to confirm/decline.

To cancel an order immediately after placing it, say **Alexa, cancel my order**

To add an item to your cart on Amazon, say **Alexa, add (item name) to my cart**.

To track your orders, say **Alexa, track my order** or say **Alexa, where is my stuff?**

Tip: To better manage your orders or contact a seller, go to amazon.com

Using Echo Dot to Get Traffic Information

You can use the Echo Dot to get information about traffic situation on your route. To get this you will first need to tell Alexa what your route is. To do this:

1. Open Alexa app and tap on the menu icon located at the top left corner of the screen.
2. Tap on **Settings**
3. Select **Traffic**
4. Enter your starting point and destination in the **From** and **To** sections by selecting **Change address**.
5. Tap **Save changes**

After this setup, you can get traffic information about your route by asking Alexa questions like:

- **Alexa, what's my commute?**
- **Alexa, what's traffic like right now?**
- **Alexa, how is my traffic**

What about Math?

Echo Dot can also help you with some mathematics and conversion. For example, you can tell Echo Dot "**Alexa, what is the square root of four?**" You may also say "**Alexa, how many centimeter are in one foot?**" or "**Alexa, what is 60 factorial**?" and so on.

Please note that you can say all the examples given above in another ways, the most important thing is to get Echo Dot to understand what you are saying.

Using Echo Dot to get definitions

You can quickly check for a meaning of a word by asking Echo Dot. For example, you may say "**Alexa, what is the meaning of flabbergasted?**"

Using Echo Dot with Wikipedia

You can use Echo Dot to get information from Wikipedia. To get Wikipedia information, say **Alexa, Wikipedia [subject]**

To tell Alexa to continue reading a Wikipedia entry, say **Alexa, tell me more.**

Using Echo to Listen to Radio Programs

Echo is integrated with internet radio service providers like TuneIn and you could actually start listening to some radio stations right this instant. You may not need to register or turn on any settings.
To start listening to radio station straightaway, you may say:

- **Alexa, play (radio station) on TuneIn.**

Using Echo Dot to Get Flash Briefing

You can use Amazon Echo Dot to get news briefing, to do this:

1. Open Alexa app and tap on the menu icon ☰ located at the top left corner of the screen.
2. Tap on **Settings**
3. Select **Flash Briefing** and then use the switch next to each item to select what you want.
4. Tap **Edit Order** to arrange when these programs play in your Flash Briefing.

After this setup, you can then hear your flash briefing using Echo Dot. To hear your flash briefing, you may say:
Alexa, what's my Flash Briefing?
Alexa, what's new?

To go back to the previous/next news, say **Alexa, previous/next.**
To stop the flash briefing, say **Alexa, cancel.**

Using Echo Dot To Get General Information

If you will like to know more about something you can ask Echo Dot. For example, you may say **Alexa, what is the shape of the earth?**

Funny sides of Echo Dot

One of the main features that that makes Echo Dot interesting is its ability to give a reply in funny manner. This all depends on what you ask it. Some of the questions you can ask it to get funny replies are given below:

- **Alexa, do you sleep?**

- **Alexa, do you eat?**

- **Alexa, do you like your job?**

- **Alexa, do you have a brain?**

- **Alexa, are you lying?**

The list of questions you can ask Echo Dot to get funny replies goes on like that. As I have said before, it all depends on the type of question you ask this device.

Echo Dot's Settings

The settings tab under Alexa app allows you to manage Echo Dot's functions. To access Alexa settings:

1. Open Alexa app and tap on the menu icon ▤ located at the top left corner of the screen.
2. Tap on **Settings**
3. Tap an option.

Tip: Settings allows to customize your Echo Dot in a special way. Whenever you think of giving your Echo Dot a special tweak, go to settings.

Troubleshooting Echo Dot

Although much efforts have been put into making this device, it is possible that Echo Dot will misbehave at one time or the other. When this happen there are few things to do.

- **Ensure that you are connected to a strong network**: If you have bad or no internet connection, Echo Dot may not work properly. Therefore the first thing to check when Echo Dot starts to misbehave is the internet connection.

- **Speak clearly in a silent place**: Make sure you are speaking clearly and try to avoid background noise. In addition, try to be specific in your commands.

- **Try to Restart Your Echo Dot**: If you find out that all what I have mentioned above does not work, you may try restarting your device. To do this, unplug your device and then plug it back after few seconds.

Resetting Echo Dot

If you have restarted your Echo Dot (by unplugging and plugging it back) but it is still misbehaving, you may try resetting your device. You may also reset your Echo Dot if you want to sell it or give it away. Please note that you will need to register it to an Amazon account and reenter any device settings to use it again after you perform a reset.

To reset your Echo Dot (2nd Generation):
- Press and hold the Microphone off and Volume down buttons at the same time until the light ring turns orange, then light ring turns blue. This may take up to 20 seconds.

- Wait for the light ring to turn off and on again. The light ring then turns orange, and Echo Dot will enter setup mode.

- Open the Alexa app to connect your device to a Wi-Fi network and register it to your Amazon account again. To learn more about setting up Echo Dot, go to page 5.

Made in the USA
Middletown, DE
13 December 2016